DROWNING

Elvis Giles

Presentation by *BookLeaf Publishing*

Web: www.bookleafpub.com

E-mail: info@bookleafpub.com

ISBN: 978-93-95755-20-7

First edition 2022

*You will find a reason, a dedication and an
inspiration in everything around you. You just
need to hear from your mind, learn from your
experiences and speak from your heart.
Sometimes even when you get a story or an
inspiration even in the middle of the night, wake
up, write it down for sometimes the spark or
light just ignited for a moment, a time being.
Grab that opportunity, that moment before it's
gone for that is your time which no one can
take it away from you. Don't let life take you
down, infact make your words so powerful that
life would bring the negative people around you
down and spread positivity among everyone
around. Remember after a storm there is always
a silence and when you listen with your heart
and speak, you find words even in that silence.*

ACKNOWLEDGEMENT

I am a self made, independent author but test I would life to acknowledge life because without my experiences and people around me I wouldn't be able to put this book together. Too many issues to address, too much to speak and too tough to break silences. My life has been a journey of these and many more experiences. This is the first of many to come and when you read it with your heart you will connect with mine for sure.

PREFACE

I am more of a romantic person but when I saw there are people who have faced a harsh or tragic experience, it's vital to bring those events into light so that those reading it may understand where they went wrong. If your going through something, these words may bring you hope and confidence and if you have faced this ordeal already you would know how far you have come. Life can be unfair sometimes and so are people. But with love and happiness, you can power come the darkest moments in yours and someone else's life. In this book I might have started off by drowning but in most of our lives the one person that saves us is our mother and that's why I ended the poem with her.

DROWNING

DROWNING

To the bully that made my high school hell,
A place where I wanted to escape from, at the
stroke of the bell,
Your words that came from your mouth were
worse than trash,
I wish someone would be there to give you a
good freaking bash,
Those endless tortures followed by a series of
bullies,
So sour that could even wither a bunch of lilies,
I was scared to get out of my room,
Scared to even go to school even if it was online
or on zoom,
Just because your height was bigger than me,
Doesn't mean picking on me should bring you
glee,
I was haunted all day and night along,
So terrified that I even forgot the lyrics of my
favourite song,
The washrooms were like a devils den, waiting
to be haunted,
Petrified, that for a moment I would imagine on
the wall, my face being mounted,

The lockers were a place where even my shadow
wouldn't go,
The world can be cruel, so little did I know,
I got shivers and chills each time someone
opened the door,
Thinking it's going to be you steaming towards
me and dragging me across the floor,
I wiped my tears, went home and cried,
Sometimes I would go to sleep even without
wiping them and let it get dried,
My eyes red, my heart pounding fast, all because
of a bully,
Each time I was in front of you I seemed to do
things that were silly,
Dreams turned into nightmares and reality into
darkness,
All I wished for a sigh of relief and cut free of
this harness,
I came home and locked my self indoors,
Like a baby crying endlessly as my tears
drenched the carpets on my floors,
Each time I tried to rise up, you pulled me back
to the ground,
The moment You came in front of me, I was
deprived of any and every sound,
I was hurt, bruised and my heart shattered,
My memories and life were all so scattered,
I would come home and lock my self indoors,

Then like a baby I would cry endlessly as the
tears even drenched the carpet on my floors,
Your worse than a fox, a hound or even an evil
snake,
How could you do this to someone and expect
them every morning to even wake,
I was a clown to you but the truth being you
were indeed a bigger one,
I just wish I would have some courage and shoot
you with a gun,
In my sorrows and miseries I kept drowning,
Drowning in a pool of agony and yet all you
could see is my clowning,
Why were you such a jerk, I just couldn't relate,
Will you stop being one? I guess that's going to
be the worlds ugliest debate,
You never did let me grow, did you,
In your eyes I was just a scary chicken, a cat
who couldn't even mew,
I came home tossed my bag and just wept
profusely,
I was called on again and again just for being
silly,
Why me mother, why? What wrong have I done,
Have I hurted someone or am i just a unlucky
son?
Those hurts ripped my hearts into pieces,
There were cheers, but it was when I was soaked
in someone's feces,

As the day turned into night all I kept was drowning,
Drowning in my misery, drowning in my sorrows, drowning in a pit knee deep I just kept drowning,
Not a hand to pick me up, not a soul to stand for me,
Perhaps picking upon me and humiliating me would fill someone else with laughter and glee,
I guess I've become a joker now, there is no hope remaining,
You would continue picking on me just like any other day and would keep on sinning,
Better then this drowning, I would rather be dead and forgotten,
But what's the fun in that as I'll be called just a joker who was once begotten,
It's ok to be sad, it's ok to cry, but it's not ok to humiliate and bully this child,
You may break him today, but for the rest of your life you will leave him insane and wild,
Give him a reason to live, give him a hope to cheer,
Don't leave him stranded drowning in a pool of his own fears,
Don't be a bully and don't stand one,
One day will come when this thing might happen to your own daughter or son,

Kids are scared and parents have no clue about
their agony,
Remember sometimes it even rains on days
which are sunny,
Help them, make them strong,
Or else they will keep forever drowning and we
will support what is wrong,
Drowning in emotion, drowning in ambition and
drowning in virtue of getting retribution,
Alas everyone is drowning somewhere thus
leading to their own destruction…..●●

- Elvis Giles ●●

YOU WILL BE FOUND

YOU WILL BE FOUND

When your weak and sometimes afraid to carry
on,
Afraid of being lost and the only person you
love being gone,
Those endless bullies, emotional tortures and
haunted memories tarnishing your fate,
But don't you worry for one day you will be
found and it will be worth the wait....

It's tough but everyday you grow stronger than
ever,
That one person, that family who loves you will
leave you never,
When your lost in the wilderness and there's no
one besides you,
You will be found by that person whom you
never even properly knew....

When your hope is depleting and there is no
more tears left to shed,
Your tears, your emotions, your pain wetting the
bed,

You will bounce back, you will survive and will
make all those haters and bullies silent,
For you will be found even when your days are
short and people around you are violent….

Be strong my friend, it's not worth it to die or
change your life when everything seems wrong,
When your weak and in doubts always
remember the words of your favourite song,
Believe in yourself, your better than you think
you are,
And one day you will be found even when you
think that the grapes have turned sour….

Life will push you just like the tides that hit the
rocks on the shores,
But there would be that one person whose love
you will forever endure,
Do not be sad, do not shed a single tear, your life
is worth a millions,
Because when that day you will be found, your
happiness will multiply in billions….

- Elvis Giles

THE UNBORN GIRL CHILD

THE UNBORN GIRL CHILD

Twisted and tangled as I lay in the womb of my mother,
Unaware, but yet eager as each day would make her grow tougher,
Little did I know she was not a boon but rather a curse,
In a society so brutal where to discriminate, one would not need to rehearse…..

As I lay there with my eyes closed, counting the days of my arrival,
How little did I know, that day would actually be one that of my burial,
The innocence with a kick or the smile that would forever fade away,
Heart broken that not a even a single word from my mouth, I would ever get to say…..

I wanted to prove to my father, I'll be the strongest girl child to be born in this male dominated crusade,

If I knew this would happen, I would tell God
not to let her girl go down and get slayed,
I didn't even get a chance to see the shinning
light or how my mother saw the world's cruelty,
But now I thank God he didn't let these savage
men destroy each day, his wonderful beauty….

I remember when they strangled me in the
womb, I had a still subtle smile on my face,
My mother in tears, yet not even able to bestow
on me her soulful grace,
Alas, as I lay there, a question flashed
constantly, which me, or no one ever had an
answer,
What was my fault mother? Why couldn't I
suffer just like her?…..

All I just wanted was a chance to experience the
pain what my mother endured,
As I faintly fell my breath being taken away
from my body and my life going blurred,
You all are murderers who should not even get a
chance to live,
I wanted to be born, but not even a single chance
for me you would give…..

Mother please don't cry, I know it's tough but
you are strong,

For so long you bore me and took care of me,
you were never wrong,
It was the society who had their hands covered
in blood and disgust,
Who had the dreams and life of this unborn girl
child forever crushed….

- Elvis Giles

YOUR HEART WILL GUIDE THE WAY

YOUR HEART WILL GUIDE THE WAY....

Life may surround you with many options and
choices,
You may get confused, dis oriented and may
even begin to hear voices,
Sometimes all we need is just silence to listen to
our heart to take the right decision,
For your heart will guide the way, while all you
just need is a firm vision....

Be strong, positive and no turning back,
Sometimes you will be put down and your days
may even get black,
You may even have a fight between your heart
and your mind,
But sometimes we just need to listen to our heart
and the right answer you will find....

Your better than you think you are,
You won't always get the sweet grapes,
sometimes they are even sour,
Your confidence in you will help you shape your
future,

If you put your heart into something, you can
scale mountains even if your an amateur....

There will be days where you think you have
lost it all,
Times when you will be passed and kicked like
an object or a ball,
Moments where your tears won't dry up and
your cries won't be heard,
Days when you will just want to be left alone
and not say a word…

What were you just thinking, you just want to
hang yourself or maybe jump off a bridge,
When you do that, all your going to do is end up
at the bottom of a fridge,
Are you curious, insensitive or maybe just a
fool,
You end your life today and that's not going to
look any cool….

In times like this, all we just need is to take a
deep breath and calm down,
You never know just this simple trick can maybe
turn into a smile from a frown,
Your heart may be broken today bruised and
shattered in a million pieces,
But each time it's broken, you will power
instead of being down, just increases…..

Life is filled with ups and downs,
Sometimes with smiles while sometimes
unending frowns,
No matter what happens, you should always
move towards your goal,
For your heart will guide you the way and bring
peace within your soul....

- Elvis Giles

YOU ARE THE LIGHT OF THE WORLD

YOU ARE THE LIGHT OF THE WORLD

Sitting there across the fire I began to wonder,
Sometimes a calm wind blows while sometimes
just being struck by thunder,
God came into this world to be ray of hope and
joy at a cost,
Making you the light of the world to lead the
souls that were once lost....

Your life is meant to give and bygones meant to
forgive,
Seeking justice for the weak and giving them a
reason to live,
It's upto us how we shape our present and
future,
For you are the light of the world, a blessing
from Mother Nature....

Abiding within the rules that were meant to
draw a line,
Asking maybe even a stranger today, 'are you
doing just fine'?

Doesn't cost a lot to even share a moment of
happiness,
When you are the light of the world, just like
God, you strive to take away all their sadness….

These thoughts may come across our minds, yet
we do nothing,
Sometimes we be lost in our thoughts just
thinking of doing something,
To change the world, you need to first change
your attitude towards the begotten,
Because when your the light of the world, the
pain they once endured will ever be forgotten….

Be kind, share the love and just be a light for
others,
Holding hand in hand standing for your sisters
and brothers,
You get only one shot to bring change into a
person's world,
And when you are their light in darkness, you
become their whole world…. 😇 ☺

- Elvis Giles  🖤

THE DARKNESS WITHIN

THE DARKNESS WITHIN

Sometimes I wonder why is it so dark outside,
And I fail to realize that actually this darkness is
within us which proactively resides,
You may be cruel, persuasive or even rude to the
one besides,
For it's this darkness which lurks within you and
then divides….

Talking ill or even putting the other person
down, may just add to someone's agony,
To the opposite person it may be haunting, while
to some it may just be funny,
Sometimes those laughters and echoes may just
tear hearts apart,
For if not removed in time, it's this darkness
which will forever pierce one's heart….

Some may show their emotions in anger, awe or
just in tears,
Some would remove their depression through
endless wines and beers,
Some would find comfort in condolences and
spontaneous cheers,

While some be lost in this darkness and get
drowned in their worst fears….

Maybe a smile or maybe even a sparkle in one's
eye,
May change someone's world even in the midst
of a thousand goodbyes,
Just like me as you sit there wandering the
goodness deep within you,
Even a small ounce of faith will forever
diminish the darkness that within you once did
brew….●●

- Elvis Giles ✸●

YOU DESERVE TO BE LOVED

YOU DESERVE TO BE LOVED

It's not been a long time we have been together,
I still thought that our relationship was strong
and not as light as a feather,
Your happiness mattered the world to me,
You deserve to be loved and kept happy, one day
you will see...

Love in words can't be expressed of how much I
have to give for you,
You were just perfect, the best from the rest
which I always knew,
The fault was in me that all I had to give you
was love without any boundaries,
To gain your love, I would even scale a thousand
countries....

You deserve to be happy, smiling and blessed
everyday,
You were the best for me always, I didn't care
what people say,
Somewhere deep within my heart for a miracle
to happen is all I pray,

For without you in my life, I don't see my future
in any way....

Your better than you think you are,
Strong, independent and happy even when we
are far,
Time is something, all I ask from you for
wounds to heal,
For when your in my life, close to family and
God I always feel....

Tears won't mean anything anymore nor will my
agony,
Love is something much more greater than even
material things or money,
Today I am nothing, but with God and you I am
everything,
For the day you realize my love for you, you
will know that this all wasn't a fling....

Even if I'm not near, I still cherish the moments
we spent together,
You always told me that you left me for my
better,
I just wish my wounded heart could be ready for
another blow,
For you deserve to be kept happy and that's all I
know....
- Elvis Giles

BROKEN NO MORE

BROKEN NO MORE

Too many nights have gone by and I still
couldn't forget,
Things that I had lost once and love which I still
couldn't get,
Life is cruel and thought me a lesson every step
of my way,
But now I'm broken no more and that's what I
have to say...

You can crush me, break me and even play with
my heart,
You don't know what you have lost today, but
will surely will know when I depart,
Too many sleepless nights and endless tears will
eventually be turned into happiness and glee,
For you were meant to teach me a lesson and not
forever be....

It's tough, but isn't that what's life all about?
Sometimes you can handle the stress, while
sometimes you just go out your window and
shout,

Love and life changes in a minute, yet we are never ready,
Ready to love someone truly, to have a relationship and life that is steady....

Broken no more you may think I am today,
Before you left, you didn't even hear what my heart had to say,
To keep you happy always is all that I will always pray,
For this is a reality and yet still I can't ever stop thinking about us every night or day....●◖

- Elvis Giles ◖●

SIMPLE THINGS WHERE HAVE YOU GONE???

SIMPLE THINGS WHERE HAVE YOU
GONE??

Times changed, seasons passed, yet we all still
live in a bubble,
Sometimes we strive, we conquer, while
sometimes we drown in our own agony of
trouble,
Times when someone would smile at you or
maybe lend out a helpful hand, now all seem to
be lost,
Sometimes I wonder, simple things where have
you gone and at what cost?….

The pure air that we used to breathe or the
prefect weather that once we all desired,
The love and joy shared by others, the good
deeds that once inspired,
Those humble moments and simple hellos that
we miss even till today,
Is now covered by masks and distance, keeping
ourselves far from what others have to say….

The peace we would experience without any
tensions or worries,
The loyalties we cherished and the genuine
apology in our meaningful sorries,
Everything's seems so lost as with time people
change so fast,
Simple things where have you gone and why
don't good times forever last…..

Life has changed and so have people around,
In this fast paced modern world we don't even
tend to look at what our world surrounds,
We just hear life is short and to make the most
out of it,
But do we take the time to look at our wrongs or
at moments when in life we quit?

Everyone has problems, but do we do
something? or just crib and cry?
Sometimes we give up so easily and we don't
even tend to try,
It's so easy these days to give up easily and put
the blame on others for our failures,
And if we don't recognize and value the simple
things in life, we will all be nothing but just
some random strangers….

Spread love and happiness, the world is too good
to be hated,

Everything that shines is not silver or gold
plated,
You live only once is what people say,
You never know for you may be the miracle for
whom someone did pray.....

Simple things where have you gone by,
Are you there in a hello, or maybe in someone's
goodbye,
So let's all bring in the cheers and raise your
glasses and cans of beers,
Don't let the simple things get lost in your
inconsolable tears....●

- Elvis Giles ●

IN THE DARKNESS COMES A LIGHT

IN THE DARKNESS COMES A LIGHT

You called out my name but I still stood there
waiting,
You said a whisper but I'm still cluelessly
debating,
How many times came by, when in the
wilderness I couldn't even see a sign of belief,
Yet I still hope that in this darkness there will
come a light that will give me a soothing
relief....

Your hand stretches out to me, but I'm just so
blinded,
Sometimes I don't even know what to speak, as
I'm not so open minded,
I know if I wait, things will turn out to be better
than before,
For when your presence embraces my life, even
wounds would heal that were once sore....

Is it true that love was all that was needed to see
one's life through?

You would always be the person who would
change my life out of the very few,
Yet I didn't let you close and didn't even give
you a chance to share my sorrows,
I still drown till today in the endless darkness
and countless nights of horrors…

Your one smile would make my misfortunes go
away,
Your one laugh would bring joy in my life at any
given night or day,
Your a ray of hope that sparkles in a pool of
inconsolable agony,
And yet in midst of this chaos your hug would
be more valuable than bags of money….

I'm still strong because you said me to be so,
You will be the person of strength whom I'll
always know,
Don't give up on me so soon, I will strive
through this endless path of failures,
For you will always be the light in the darkness
of my life, my angel, my saviour….●●

- Elvis Giles ●●

THE LIFE IN A HEARTBEAT

THE LIFE IN A HEART BEAT

Every micro second, our heart beats,
Even though we don't count, it keeps on beating
and does not even cheat,
Yes, the biological expressions of heart are quite
practical,
Indeed the life in a heart beat cannot be
explained for the feeling is just magical..

Have you ever realized we are alive because of
our heart,
Some may have a bitter while some may be a
sweet heart,
We do say that my heart always beats for you,
But do you realize that if it stops, there will be
no more me and you..

Its only when you die, you understand the
importance of a heart beat,
Dhak dhak it goes as though its so mechanical
and sweet,
One beat gives you another chance to live,
Another moment, another expression to give..

The heart is just a piece of an instrument,
It is God who always keeps on playing the
melody, so fluent,
God never gets tired of playing anytime,
For he gives us the sweetest beats in our life all
the time..

If humans were without a heart, there wouldn't
be love,
If there was no heart beat, there wouldn't be any
life,
It would be difficult in this world to even
survive,
And the moment it starts beating, only a miracle
can keep you breathing and have you revived….

The life in a heart beat can't be explained,
It may be magical and sometimes so very faint,
Sometimes you may use a stethoscope to hear a
heart beat,
But you can't use a microscope to see the life in
a heart beat..🎧💿

-Elvis Giles 🖤🖤🖤

MIXED EMOTIONS

MIXED EMOTIONS

Sitting there wondering just like any other one,
what has life done for me?
Is this what I wanted, or is it just meant to be,
Sometimes being sad and worried,
Sometimes just thinking of the day when In
ashes I'll be buried…..

Not everyday is one like this, sometimes it's just
filled with happiness,
Smiles and laughter that drive me out of every
wilderness,
After every darkness, there is a ray of light,
And sometimes my emotions get the better out
of me and It turns out to an unwanted fight….

Like a crazy person, sometimes I'll sit there just
smiling,
Sometimes just day dreaming or sometimes just
grumbling and whining,
Sometimes falling in love with something and
getting lost or flustered,
Then coming back to reality and regretting the
decisions I once had mastered….

So many emotions yet no words left to say,
Changing across people and faces every night
and day,
With love and care all we have to do is put our
heart out there sometimes,
For mixed emotions may get the best out of you
this time but not everytime....😎●

- Elvis Giles 🖤●

OUT OF THE DARKNESS

OUT OF THE DARKNESS

I stood there wandering in the darkness,
A darkness that made me hollow, something that
made me tied by a harness,
I cried, I wept I was totally shattered,
Filled in agony, despise and staying away from
things that mattered....

Searching for a smile, for a ray of hope,
Trying to remove the dirt from me which didn't
come out even with water and soap,
Why is that, the world is cruel and I'm afraid,
Afraid that I may die unhappy and scared....

My eyes wept profusely, my heart lost in the
wilderness,
No body beside me, nobody to be my witness,
Will there be a helping hand that comes walking
from the door,
Will there be an angel from above, who will
change my life sweeping my legs off the floor....

Too many things that trouble me and cover my
shadow,

Trying to move on, just trying to be happy and
to grow,
What is that I must do to find peace and love,
What is it that God wants, what does he want me
to serve?

Heart breaks are wounds that can be healed but
scars will remain,
Some that will make me ponder on and some
that will drive me insane,
We need to be strong, but a voice within us
holds us back,
For to come out of this darkness , pure love is all
that we lack....

I kept screaming but everyone turned on a blind
eye,
I didn't want to go anywhere, just scared to even
say goodbye,
If we don't go out today, tomorrow will be ready
to haunt us forever,
For out of this darkness we will need to come as
it's going to be now or never....●●

- Elvis Giles 💔●

TIMES CHANGE

TIMES CHANGE

Just when I thought everything would be alright,
it changed,
There seems to be something missing even when
smiles are exchanged,
People get busy, not everyone will have time for
you,
But be strong for times change and also people
whom you once knew....

It doesn't take a minute to bid goodbye to
someone,
Not knowing if that person will come back or
you just might be done,
Times don't stay good always, nor they may stay
bad,
For times do change and all it takes is that one
moment to be happy from being sad....

Have faith, be strong, your time won't stay the
same forever,
All you need is that one person to hold your
hand and stay with you now and ever,

We need to learn to get happiness from the little
things in life that we come across,
Yes indeed times do change and you never know
when you become their boss....

Hope is something that you need to strive on and
never loose,
We are God's people and sometimes, to do his
work, as a median we may be used,
You may not have anything to give today to the
opposite person,
But your time won't stay the same and if you
stay strong nor will it anytime worsen.... ☺

- Elvis Giles

NO ONE IS PERFECT

NO ONE IS PERFECT

I may have done mistakes which I regret,
Decisions and actions which I can't forget,
My life was filled with love and happiness ever
since you I've met,
My love for you was purely true and that I can
always bet....

I know I've hurted you, cursed you and even
broken your heart,
A promise was broken, a promise never to
depart,
You were my life, my everything, my
sweetheart,
For your beautiful, intelligent, sweet and
smart....

I'm sorry for the hurts and wounds I've given
you,
Sorry for not being able to understand you and
putting you in blue,
You were the definition of love, of life, that I
always new,

I don't want a chance, just an opportunity to
prove myself like the morning dew....

I won't and can't promise anything I can't fulfill,
Not just in words, but with deeds I will do your
will,
If you leave me, I will stand there waiting still,
For I'm not perfect, but your life with happiness
I will fill....●●

- Elvis Giles ●●

A VALENTINES STORY

A VALENTINES STORY

There was a day he met her and to him, she was
the perfect one,
Even though she was a girl, she was stronger
than any man or son,
She was beautiful, god fearing, just the one he
was looking for,
The day he met her he told that he was forever
yours....

They were a cute couple and everybody loved
them,
She had the purest of hearts, more valuable than
any gold or gem,
Her love was pure but times changed,
He make mistakes and said words which made
her feel chained....

Times went by, he still couldn't stop loving her,
Her touch, her love, her beauty, those times
when together they were,
A miracle he was longing for, he prayed
earnestly to God everyday,

But for her happiness and to keep her happy
always, he prayed every night and day....

Love is all that somebody can give sometimes,
Times change, they can be sometimes sweet as
honey and sometimes sour like limes,
Relationships shouldn't be just one day, two or
only Valentine's,
When you love that person truly, you will
always pay attention to all her signs....

This story may be yours, mine or any body who
reads this,
Our true partner, our other half, even if they do
mistakes we will always miss,
Let's not make love live just one day,
For let this Valentine's Day be yours and your
God to whom you always pray....●●

- Elvis Giles ♥

WHEN YOU ARE DOWN

WHEN YOU ARE DOWN

When you are down I look unto you,
The person who is closest to me the person I
always knew,
You seem to take away all my worries, stress
and anxieties,
You will always find me with you in any town or
cities....

You are a strong person with a personality unlike
others,
You seem to get away from people that makes
you bother,
Your beautiful, with a good heart mind and soul,
To keep you happy will always be my ultimate
goal....

You are sad today, tomorrow a smile will curve
through the darkness,
In the days to come, your life is going to be
filled with blessings and happiness,
You are God's child and he won't let you go
astray,

For to keep you always happy and successful is
all that I pray....

Your life may be messed up today but won't be
the same tomorrow,
I'm here for you always to take away all your
sorrows,
To make you smile I will go the ends of the
world,
I just have my heart to give you more valuable
than any silver or gold....

I failed to understand you at first,
Your anger your stress ultimately did burst,
I'm a human not perfect but a soul with purity,
Your the greatest gift I've got and I'm sorry I've
dealt it with immaturity....

When you are down, I am down with you too,
When you are stressed, my heart weeps for you,
You don't know how much you mean to me and
what you are,
For your truly a gem who can turn sweet even
people that are sour...●●

- Elvis Giles● ●

AMONG THE SHADOWS

AMONG THE SHADOWS

You've stood there waiting all this long in
darkness,
I was somewhere far but under some type of
harness,
You kept on calling, some heard but couldn't do
anything,
For among the shadows you sored and still
couldn't say a thing...

After every dark night comes a day shining so
bright,
When I share my feelings with you, my heart
feels so light,
Your heart is wounded but with proper love can
be healed,
For among the shadows lies all your answers
enclosed in a heart that is sealed...

Time will not stay the same forever, it will
change for the better,
All those times you spend endless nights that
we're sour and bitter,

There will come a time when someone like me
will come to rescue you,
From the shadows true love will win, time and
again when that person pulls you out of the
blue...

Your smile can drive a million troubles away,
To see you happy there is no value on earth that
one could pay,
So cheer up, be glad, your days of sadness are
coming to an end,
For its through these shadows you will find your
angel whom God has sent.... ☺

- Elvis Giles

A JOURNEY OF GOOD SOULS

A JOURNEY OF GOOD SOULS

Born from dust, nurtured and raised,
Brought into a world where each time we are
truly amazed,
We were born as humans, but we leave this
world as a soul,
Some may be good, some bad while some just
not enough to make you whole....

After death, we all debate what life would be
perhaps,
Some enjoy paradise, while some are held
accountable for all their mishaps,
A good soul's journey may be tough but not
impossible,
Because with God by your side, even a prodigal
son's journey to heaven can be made possible..

Do good is all we hear from God and his
teachings,
We learn things the hard way, when we tend to
deny his preachings,

Sometimes even good people suffer while the bad strive,
But ultimately it's the journey of these good souls that keep the good in this world alive.... 😇 ☺

- Elvis Giles ●●

LET THERE BE LIGHT

LET THERE BE LIGHT

As the sun dawns and the night shadows you,
As the times darkness prevails amongst the good
times that are few,
Shadows your life and degrades your inner you,
Burdening yourself and keeping yourself locked
away from the people you once knew....

A ray of Hope is all you need,
In a stock of hay, all you need is faith as small as
a seed,
Life may kick you a million times but you have
to stay strong,
For if you don't, all you tend to take is decisions
that are wrong....

God is there you may know but not believe,
He only gives you trouble how much you can
take under your sleeve,
Once you seek help to him, he will answer you
in the form of a miracle,
For he is written your faith and can make your
life something magical....

He was the one who created you and the
universe,
He can set you free from any wrong doings or
any curse,
A ray of light that shines your life that will come
in your time of dispair,
For even enemies are changed when they say a
truthful and thankful prayer...😇 ☺

- Elvis Giles 🙏⚫

MY MOTHER

MY MOTHER

I remember when I was a small and an innocent
kid,
I was told by my teacher to write a few words on
'My Mother',
I gladly wrote, but what made me sad was that I
failed to repay you for all that you did,
For your love is unconditional mom and unlike
any other....

How can someone be so beautiful in both in
body and soul,
How can someone love so much that even the
stars in the sky would seem less,
How can someone dedicate their whole life to
keep others happy and make a family whole,
For she is my mother, whom God from above
has always blessed....

Sometimes I left you alone and didn't even see
your there,
Ignorance and stubbornness, all I did was put
you in despair,

Maybe father thinks that you are a blessing to
him by being his wife,
But he is wrong, as you are the foundation and
centre of all in our life...

So many words but it still seems so incomplete,
Your love is endless but my words would still
seem less,
So much mercy and compassion, in your every
step in every heart beat,
Like an angel sent from above, which God has
blessed...

I may be in tears as I write you these words,
I'm sorry for the times I failed to be a good and
obedient son,
My mother, my life, I can't tell you how much I
love you in just these words,
But I'll strive each day of my life to keep you
happy and love you a ton...

Mother of mine how sweet and pure you are,
With your love, you can even turn things sweet
from sour,
Even though I may be far from you today,
My love for you will remain the same now,
forever, everyday....

- Elvis Giles

www.ingramcontent.com/pod-product-compliance
Lightning Source LLC
LaVergne TN
LVHW021249200726
843509LV00012B/1617